Chasing Grace

Katheryn Rios

Chasing Grace

Copyright © 2018 by Katheryn Rios

All rights reserved.

Dedication

To Carolyn,

You are my strength! You are my person! You created this beautifully flawed warrior. I love you mom.

To Alexis Maldonado,

I never got to meet you but you would've been so proud of me. Sleep in peace, biggest brother.

To Daniel Rios,

I promised your memory would live on.

Sleep in peace Tio.

Table Of Contents

TRIGGER WARNINGS

Chapter 1: Breaking the statistics

Chapter 1.5: Dear, You- Not a battle but a Letter

Chapter 2: An Unfortunate Event

Chapter 3: Two angry men

chapter 3.5: Bang- Battle #1

Chapter 4: Night of terror

Chapter 5: Black Wave

Chapter 5.5: Loss- Battle #2

Chapter 6: Exchange

Chapter 6.5: Blackout- Battle #3

Chapter 7: H.I.M

Chapter 7.5: Solitude- Battle #4

Chapter 8: Changes

Chapter 8.5: Young girl, don't cry- Battle #5

Chapter 9: What have I done?

Chapter 9.5: I don't love you like i loved you yesterday- Battle #6

Chapter 10: This is now

Chapter 10.5: Not sober anymore- Battle #7

Chapter 11: Hello friend's

Chapter 12: A familiar face

<u>Chapter 12.5: Wake me up when it's over- Battle #8</u>

Chapter 13: The end or beginning?

Index

The characters portrayed in this book are fictitious or are used fictitiously. Any similarity to real people is coincidental, and not intended by the author.

The events in this book are based on true life events.

TRIGGER WARNINGS:

Mental abuse

Physical abuse

Cheating

Lying

Rape

Sex

P.T.S.D

Self-harm

Depression

Anxiety

Miscarriage

Anger management

Abandonment

Drugs

Manipulation

Child Abuse

Chapter 1:

Breaking the statistics

I look back and think to myself; if I was brought up not knowing any better towards the way I looked at what was right and what was wrong, was it because of the life I was given? It seemed perfectly normal for me being raised in the Bronx and being a part of the system. By the system I mean public assistance. Let's be honest who wouldn't appreciate food stamps on a monthly basis, and other free shit that helped us get by every day. It was secure, and comfortable for a while. Besides I wasn't the one dealing with the paperwork and all that extra crap. Thanks mom.

As you know we all have to grow up sometime, and that time is now. I had children of my own and my whole perspective changed. I stopped to think that at some point in this misery we call life I became unhappy, and this really wasn't the life I wanted. This wasn't how my life was supposed to be. I knew nothing of right or wrong, and I had to change it. Reality hit me when I had nothing to offer my children. No home of my own, no job, and barely an education. What could someone like me possibly have to offer three innocent kids? I was still a kid myself. I was following the same exact patterns of my family. Depending on fucking welfare.

I decided to make the first move and come out of my comfort zone for good. Shit, did that backfire quickly. I basically got hit with "so you thought you'd prosper in life? think again kid" by society. Apparently, my life didn't adjust well to change. I had to make it clear that I was in control. How the hell was I supposed to do that?

September of 2015, I remember it like yesterday. It was the most exciting yet heartbreaking damn year of my life. For once I finally decided to do something productive with my life. I was tired of depending on shit just to get my kids and I by. I was tired of feeling like shit because a man would look at me and say they could never be with a single mother on welfare who hadn't even finished school. My heart shattered each time I heard how worthless I was.

One day I broke down in tears and a fire sparked in me. A spark by the name of Anita. I was inspired and motivated to get some part of my life together with her encouragement. Anita was my child's therapist but in the process she changed me. Anita showed me that nothing was impossible. I finally found the moral support to help me take the next steps to better my life. Anita helped me obtain my Diploma, and it was the most incredible feeling ever. The day I passed my exam it felt as if the entire world froze, and I knew that everything was gonna be ok.

For some odd reason at that time I couldn't help but picture my parent's reaction in my head though. They were never really supportive of my achievements, goals, and dreams growing up. I guess they didn't know how to be, or I guess they never believed that I would make it out of poverty. If they couldn't make it themselves, how could I? Don't get me wrong, my parents love me but they sure had a strange way of showing it.

The Lost man was a love from far away or when he needed my emotional support. There's a bunch of difunctional shit in our relationship but that's a whole other chapter in itself. My mom was a love that was meant to teach us lessons. In my mother's eyes, everything she did was for the greater good or to protect us from committing horrible mistakes. Basically, she tried to protect us from the mistakes she made. I don't blame her. My mother went through a rough patch herself.

Everything I did in life, I second guessed, and I always felt I was never good enough for one sometimes both of them. Let's be honest if you don't have your own mother, or Lost man's moral support how could you possibly move forward in life?

In the late 1980's my mom, and the Lost man met. They were honestly the worst couple in the world, but that's in my opinion. My mom comes from a family of nine, in which she was the oldest. My mom was a brilliant, beautiful, talented, and driven young girl, but of course her childhood was shortened when she had to play the role of a second mom to my uncles, and aunts.

Quickly my mom took the responsibilities of her younger siblings alongside my teen grandmother at the time. Mom was beyond her age in knowledge and experience when it came to raising kids. There was really never any stability with different men coming into her life as father figures. That cycle continued into her love life when she met her spouse at the age of 13.

Now in that time teen pregnancy was huge in the Latino community. So of course, my mom thought she was in love with her boyfriend at the time and eventually she got pregnant, and they married. My mother was only

14 years old when she had her first child, but for reasons we can't explain, it just wasn't his time. God rest his soul. A few years later my mom moved on from her loss, and she eventually had my now older brother Abi at the age of 18. After came the beautiful Grace, me at 19, and lastly my younger brother Frenchy at 22. My mom, and the Lost man were so young, and married for all the wrong reasons. They strongly believed in marriage due to pregnancy. This marriage was broken even before it began.

    My mother did everything in her power as a teen mom to provide the best life she could with the resources she was given on her own. Public Assistance, Housing, and Section 8 in New York City was booming at that time. So, she took full advantage, and got us stable. Now that's what you call a fighter. For 21 years of my life my mother took care of us the best that she could. Sadly, she followed her mother's example of different unstable relationships throughout the years in hopes that she could find real love.

So, where does that leave me you may ask? Well, I'm now a mother of three beautiful children. So much for breaking the statistics right? I guess you can say I decided to change the cycle a little bit at least. I am now a full-time student in college with a semester left until I receive my Associates degree. How does that fit in all of this crazy history? Well, I will be the first in my family to attend, and graduate college. Although I am currently on public assistance myself I am fighting to revolt against all the odds, and seriously trying to break these damn statistics.

Now, back to 2015. The actual story in which my life began to change. It was November, and the holidays were starting to approach. It was my first time celebrating alone. I was so used to my home being festive, and full of joy. People knocking on our door asking for mom's pasteles, and coquito. It was truly an empty and depressing time for me that year.

At that time my mother left our home, and moved away before we could even say goodbye. There was a lot of personal shit she was enduring behind closed doors, and she hid it well. New York was draining her and she wanted out. A fresh start I guess you can say, so to the sunshine state she fled. Florida. For me, that's where my troubles began.

Mom was never great at finding a love that deserved her. So, when she told me she had found "the one" I was quite skeptical. I guess if that's what made her happy then so be it right? I was always the type to fight my mom's battles, and defend her against any harm, but this battle was one I couldn't win, because this time she was in love, and you know what that shit does to you. Love is seriously fucking blinding.

Fast forward to now. It was the best decision she made. This man helped my mom seek a love beyond us all. God.

Chapter 1.5:

Dear, You- Not a battle but a letter

You, you never put as much interest in my life, as you have with your other seed. You only look for me in your time of loneliness, or when you needed emotional support because your relationship wasn't going as planned. It was always supposed to be the other way around. Yet you dismissed me. You never asked me about my pain. You never showed me the love that a man is supposed to give me, setting me up for failure in the long run. For years I've watched you put others before me. I'd stare out of my bedroom window waiting for a broken promise that never was kept. I grew more and more resentment inside of me with each lie you planted in me. You watered this anger with my tears of disappointment when you let her take away all of the time we could've had together. How could you let her speak badly of us? How could you let her try to destroy an image of our mother? How dare you let her speak badly of our mother when she was the other woman who destroyed your marriage? How could you let her degrade us in such a way? How could you let her belittle us, and beat us when we were just children, and innocent? You have never defended us, and because of that I will never feel good enough. Because of you I don't believe that a man isn't capable of leaving his family. How could I, when you abandoned me! I've tried for your love over, and over again. The day that you disowned Abi, and I publicly on social media for everyone to see was the day that I gave up trying. Abi will always take your place as my savior. You never cease to disappoint me. After all of the attempts at trying to earn your love; I'm letting go of you because holding on is only destroying me. You shame me yet again, and speak to me as if I'm just another stranger on the street. Is it because I am the spitting image of what you lost, and could never have again? Or is it because you can not face the truth? Tell me, is this a lie? Did you not say I wasn't yours? That you only have one child. The only liar here has always been YOU! You have failed us. You were supposed to protect, and love us. Yet the one thing you did was sit down, and watched us endure the abuse. What kind of person does such a thing? And all for what? A love that doesn't exist anymore? You will always pick her over us. I'm done. All I feel is disappointment, pain, sadness, and depression as I write this letter to you. You will never have the chance to know me again. So, this is for the password journal I asked you for at age nine that you gifted me at twenty-one. For the digital camera I begged for year after year, and the scrubs I added to my student loans because you wouldn't answer my text the week I started college. This is for the love I never got in return and the simple things in life I lost because you couldn't find it in you to be a man. Thank you!

Best Wishes,

Grace the BITCH; as you called me.

Chapter 2:

An Unfortunate Event

My kids and I had a simple routine. We were finally settling in at home. We had no care in the world of what was to come. I mean we weren't perfect, but we were happy. School had started for all of us. We were up to date on doctor visits, social outings and grades were looking amazing. Of course, lifes challenges would hit at a time so peaceful. Everything suddenly changed.

One day I woke up to a hard knock on my door. It was a man searching for my mother. This man explained that he was there on behalf of the housing court. I never knew such a place existed. I mean I've never heard of it, and I never dealt with our apartment. It was always my mother. I figured if I had the rent paid everything was ok. Boy, was I fucking wrong.

In all of our years living in this place I still couldn't grasp my mother finally giving up, and leaving.

My mother has always been fighting her way around poverty. The only life I knew was a low income one. We lived under housing for low income families, but my mother always did her best to make sure we had our home, food, and something clean to wear.

So, in August of 2015 everything began to take a toll for the worse. All the support, and help my mother was receiving officially had gotten cut off. A bill of over 2,000 dollars was now due, and she was gone. I was alone with no job, three children, and in my first semester of College. How the fuck was i gonna get 2,000 dollars?

The letter stated that if the payment was not received within three days prior to the date it was received, we would have to be seen in court, and an eviction would be issued. My heart immediately sank. The only home that I've known for over 20 years now was slipping right before my eyes, and I had no knowledge or information on how to go about this situation.

I'm a stubborn girl full of pride, so I never asked anyone for help. There wasn't a damn thing I could do, and I felt like screaming my lungs away. I remember my heart began to race, and tears were just pouring from all sides of my face. All I could think about was my children, and what would happen now. Where would we go? I thought about school. Now I would have to drop out. I had no one to turn to. Anxiety soon clouded my thoughts, and all I could do was feel sorry for my kids and I.

Later that day I tried looking into some options I thought I might have. I called my mother, and I could never forget the first thing she said to me. As she spoke to me so nonchalantly, and calm she explained that I'd figure it out, and that I could go into a shelter. For a while I was pretty devastated, hurt, and angry with her. I couldn't understand why this was happening to me. I completely removed all communications with her. I just couldn't comprehend all of it and needed to be alone. So I kept my distance and let my depression consume me.

After a while I couldn't stand the thought of not having my mother involved in my life. So, I had to learn to move forward, and forgive her. It was a long process because I refused to accept that she didn't owe me an explanation. The truth is no one owes you anything in this life; it's how we choose to go about it that determines who we are. I was now a mother of three. A college student, and no longer a little girl.

Granted things could've been dealt with differently but who are we to say what way is right or what way is wrong. My mother did the best she could with limited resources, limited knowledge, and help. It was time for me to grow up and take responsibility on my own.

Then is when I truly learned of her motives, and the reason why she suddenly left in such despair. I never questioned her again. Honestly, it broke my heart to hear what she was experiencing behind closed doors.

How could I not see the signs? How was it possible that the woman I looked up to was slipping right beneath me into these mean streets? So she ran, and she ran as far, and as fast as she could.

My mother would've probably been lost, sick or dead today. This fast paced city full of violence, and drugs was slowly consuming our neighborhood, and it wasn't long until it reached our front door. My mother was losing herself.

Unfortunate events occur in one's life all the time, and sometimes we can't do a damn thing to stop it from occurring but we can overcome it in time. We can rise above it. It's been the hardest road to walk on my own. Accepting things in my life that I can not change or even have control over. Fighting with these thoughts, just playing over in my head. It became time consuming, and later on spread like wildfire. Eating away at me like a parasite in my head. All I could do was continue to move forward and know that this pain was temporary. Everything has an expiration date.

I remember the first time I went into the shelter. I was alone with all my kids, a stroller, and a suitcase. The eviction had already taken place. I had given away everything I had. I was so new to all of this. I was afraid, and let's not forget I was embarrassed. People tend to look at you with this disappointment on their face, like if you chose to be in this predicament.

Well I don't know about other people, but I sure as hell did not want to be there. I must have cried for about an hour straight; inside of a fast food restaurant before I finally built up the courage to walk into that intake center for the homeless. That night we went through metal detectors, and waited about an hour in a line just to be asked, "what's the reason you're here?" my response was, "Is this the intake center for the homeless? I thought I saw a sign by the detectors saying that." At that point, the caseworker could hear the sarcasm in my voice. I didn't give a damn anymore. I was over it, and I just wanted my old home back.

It's crazy how when you're placed in such a situation you tend to really appreciate every moment of the past. I wish I could've just turned back time, and hugged the walls of my home once more. I wish I could've just taken in every moment, and just thanked God for a chance to be living in such a peaceful, and clean home. Everything inside of me was breaking to pieces, and I couldn't do anything but move forward.

I took a deep breath, and I prepared myself for this horrible night. It was a process of chasing after my son who was diagnosed with Autism, and ADHD while trying to maintain my girls from being afraid, and crying. I had to make sure they were as comfortable as possible. Then another process of running up, and down the elevators to different floors we were being sent to. These people probably asked me the same questions in a million different ways for about 4 hours straight. This had to be some kind of joke.

    Finally a damn break.

    They called my name at the lower level for an overnight stay. Another 2 hour wait just to find a place to sleep that night. We were placed in a foreign building with no food, no blankets, and no toiletries. Thank God I grabbed about three bags of that intake food. I was exhausted at this point, and I really didn't give a shit. I just wanted some sleep. It was 3am when I fed my kids a bologna sandwich with mustard. Stale carrots with ranch dressing, and a milk carton. I was just grateful they had some type of food to eat. I wrapped my kids up with the largest sweaters I could find in my suitcase and they were finally fast asleep.

    I remembered just laying down, and closing my eyes. It literally felt like twenty minutes later, and a knock on my door woke me up. There I was again preparing my kids, and at 6am to return back to that hell hole. Before we were done I could remember just crying my ass off again for the millionth time wishing the nightmare would be over soon. Breathing; and sucking it up I went back for another whole process of metal detectors, and waiting on line. Then more waiting to be called and asked a million of the same damn questions again. What a fucking headache.

Finally, a placement was given to us at 9pm. "Brooklyn?" You gotta be shitting me. I had to keep my composure. Everything I know, and all of my things were here in the Bronx. What was I going to do alone in Brooklyn with 3 kids, and barely any money or food?

We waited another two hours for a van that picked us up, and two other families. We arrived in this strange place I've never seen before. I was just glad to be alone at last so I could finally have time to recover and breathe as my kids slept. I brought along some extra snack bags from the shelter, and a bunch of milk cartons. At least it would hold us down for about two days. Our first night alone. The wait to see if I'd be approved to stay beyond 10 days began.

Unfortunately that same night would be my last night there. I remember washing myself with a sample of a body wash I kept in our suitcase, and drying myself with an old T-shirt I had. I finally dropped next to my daughter on the bunk bed they had already set up in the apartment. All of the kids were asleep. I just remembered looking at my daughter and saying sorry while rubbing her sweet innocent little face. It was the first night I could finally get some real sleep or so I thought.

My daughter woke up screaming, and crying. At that point I was freaking out. I had no idea what was wrong with her. I turned on the light, and of course to my surprise my daughter is filled with insect bites, bed bug bites to be precise. Apparently she was allergic.

That night I rushed her, and my two other kids to the emergency room. When will I get a fucking break?

I was in complete shock, and disappointment. Just knowing I would have to return to that damn intake center. All I could do was cry in frustration. I was filled with anger. So, I headed on the train back to the Bronx with my kids. The kids were completely exhausted. This was the last straw for me.

I threw in the towel that same day, and I no longer had the strength in me to keep fighting. Sacrifices would now be made. I called my last option. My youngest daughter's father, and I begged to stay with him for a while. I knew it'd come back around to bite me in the ass one day. I needed stability for my kids.

Calling Carson was one of my greatest mistakes, but as a desperate mother I had no other options, and my kids needed a home. Next stop, Camden, New Jersey.

I thought Pontiac, Michigan was a shit hole. That was an understatement. Camden was the most ghetto, and ratchet city I had ever been in. Houses full of graffiti and dogs running loose on every other five blocks or so. Crackheads feening to get high roaming the streets. Bullets, and arguing emerging almost every night. I wanted nothing to do with life outside of a new home full of strangers.

I was grateful Carson's family took us in but it wasn't my home and it made me more depressed. I had no one. Not a friend or someone to comfort me. Carson was being consumed by pills and leaving me abandoned in a room to myself everyday. I wanted nothing more but to scream, and run away. I had nowhere else to go.

Each day that passed our relationship as parents worsened. We were no longer a couple and yet sex overshadowed that. He used me. Night after night I was locked inside of this room. Isolated from the others with just my kids. I barely ate because everything was on a strict schedule with so many people living in the home. Soon my depression contributed to my lack of eating.

I no longer owned a phone at this point, and I lost all connection with the world for about a week straight. My son began feeling like an outsider and was forced to eat or play on a strict schedule. Even the use of a Television was limited to an hour a week. Showers were no more than five minutes at a time. Meals were twice a day with no snacks. It wasn't that way for everyone in the household though. It was complete torture compared to what we were accustom to. Until Nina found me.

Nina is my first, and closest cousin. We've always looked out for one another. Nina I'd say is the sister I never had growing up. Nina has always been a soulmate for me. So when she didn't hear from me after a week she feared the worst. Soon Police appeared at the home that I was residing in, and that was my way out. I felt a relief knowing someone out there was looking for me.

It wasn't long after my uncle came to my rescue, and drove two hours back home to New York. Nina, my aunt, and grandma took us in. Of course they asked why I didn't turn to them when I needed help. You know how that goes. We never want to be a burden. Without hesitation they took us all in. At last I felt a sense of peace and safety. After a week I spoke to my mom and booked us tickets to Florida. She agreed on letting me stay with her until I could get back on my feet. I was back to square one depending on my mom once again. Screw it, at least we're safe.

The day I packed and got ready to leave was one of the most heartbreaking days of my life. Saying goodbye to Nina was hard for me since she was my only sense of peace. It would now be a long distance relationship with my soulmate. Back to Misery. Back to the disappointments. Back to reality.

Chapter 3:

Two Angry Men

Carson is the father of my youngest daughter. Our relationship was just all over the place. Originally we started dating and just having fun. I wasn't looking for a serious commitment, just something to pass my time. We both got caught in our hidden adventures, and eventually I got pregnant. We all know when you chose to be with someone you didn't love because of a child it's just gonna be a shit show of drama, and that's exactly what it was.

I tried being a good girlfriend but he was consumed by insecurities and doubt. Carson believed that I could never really love him so he continued on with other relationships. I loved him for the man he was, and all he'd done, but it wasn't true love. It was a love for being the amazing father he is to Violet-Ann. Something my Lost man never was. So, we went our separate ways.

Seth was in a completely different environment. Seth was my first relationship in which I experienced Domestic Violence. At that time I didn't know what that meant. I thought I was always the problem with wanting to be loved and feeling good enough. Maybe I was, but Seth had demons of his own he was battling with.

Carson, and Seth really did a number on me and it was now something that consumed my mind. For a while I believed It was only me causing the outburst. I tend to attract the same men in my life. The same situations keep occurring, so it must've been me. I was clearly doing something wrong.

Seth was my first relationship heartbreak, but I was more in love with the idea of having him. It was the sex that held me longer in that relationship. He would make me feel as if I were worthless to just come right back around, and give me pleasure while telling me how much he loved me. I was caught in his web of lies. Every time he would hit me he'd make it ok because he'd fix that right up by spreading my legs and sexually satisfying me, or he'd take me on dates.

There was never closure or answers to why he'd lash out on me and it began consuming me. Questions emerged in every argument like "Why don't you love me?" or "Why me?" Seth wanted everything his way and any other way was unacceptable for him. Everyone made it clear that I was at fault because at times my thoughts would be to much to bare decreasing my interest for sex with him. Eventually, he'd get aggressive and began choking me when I argued to be loved. So, he decided to cheat more, and more each day that passed. Until one day I no longer had the strength to continue on. I ran away never to see him again.

I needed a new life in a new State. Pontiac, Michigan. That's where I met Carson. I was a single mother of two at that time, just trying to make a living when I left Seth. It was hard but it wasn't impossible.

I had the support of some family members. I had new friends, and a new job.

I moved in with Carson, as he worked hard to support our family. There were days that I felt I was going crazy. I could no longer work and I hid my pregnancy in fear of judgement. I was having a child with a man I barely knew, and Within an adventure that started off two months prior to moving. What have I done? This man was a complete stranger, and not the father of my other two children.

The months that past were full of torment and torture. I had no one once I left with Carson and I was completely isolated in a state I knew nothing of. That winter in Pontiac would be one of the coldest winters I've known. Blackouts and Black ice completely surrounded us. Not only was it cold outside but inside of our home as well. The bickering, and fights began. Eventually I found myself changing into this monster.

Each time a new girl would pop up in his messages I would resent him more. Each day he would come home late. My hate only grew stronger. The lies began taunting me. I hated him for not knowing me, and not taking care of me at my worst and most vulnerable state. I hated him for being so cold with my fragile heart.

My anger only grew stronger at that point and I began to hurt him with objects. Throwing anything I found towards him everytime he lied. I felt like a damn fool. I wanted to hurt him just so he could feel the pain I was feeling. My anger overwhelmed me. I couldn't understand how a man could cause so much misery with his unborn child growing inside of me.

Even trying to hurt him never satisfied me so eventually I pretended to be happy, and forced myself to stop caring until my baby was born. Carson lost me and didn't even realize it. Carson began feeling the neglect and distance in our relationship and it only made him angier. I lost all love and interest in him as if he meant nothing to me.

The stress was causing me to lose weight during my pregnancy so I went into premature labor. I hated him more for that. Then finally a light in this darkness I was living in. My baby was born. My Beautiful, and healthy Violet-Ann. For a while the pain numbed, and melted away. Violet-Ann took all of it away.

Over time it became rough living in Pontiac, and our situation only worsened. We decided to move back in with my Mom in New York. Now I'm taking you back to my life in New York with Carson along my side. How I just stopped caring. Everything in me turned cold and that was the ending to a relationship that clearly was shit.

Nightlife entered my world. I began running away from my problems at home. Every weekend I'd meet up with my friend Sara or my cousin Nina. We'd party our lives away, and I loved every minute of it. I could drink and forget about the pain for that night until our weekends began turning into weekdays.

I was losing myself to liquor, parties, and pills. Anything to get away from him. Anything to forget the pain. Only to wake up the next day in misery once more. I fell deeper, and deeper into the abyss.

The day finally arrived. The day in which I reached my breaking point. Carson had pushed me to the edge starting yet another argument. He was desperate for me to love him once again.

That night I began punching holes on my door. My anger took control of me. I screamed that i could no longer take this torture. I screamed that I hated him and wished I never met him. At that point my mom stepped in, and told me to take a walk to cool off. She could tell I was about to explode, and so I left.

Who would've known that my anger that night would push me close to my death.

Chapter 3.5:

Bang- battle #1

Take a few breaths, inhale and exhale for a second, and now reload. The countdown begins 3,2,1 BANG, BANG we're at it again. The holes on the door, the broken mirrors and walls, I can't take this. I feel like breaking it all down. This constant reminder. I admit I fucked up. I should've never gone through your shit and bugged you about it. Maybe I created the monster. I thought you loved me. Maybe I deserve all this shit for being a little bitch about our love and shouting "why don't you love me? Why aren't you satisfied with me? Am I not good enough? Tell me. What am I doing wrong? I can do better. Please fix me, so that I can be perfect for you." I don't understand. How could you love her, and not me? I am the woman who held your seed. Do I deserve this for sticking around while we were unhappy? The screaming in my body, aches in my heart. Replaying everything over and over and over again. My fucking mind is spinning. Why can't I let it go? Is it because the memories surround me? Just thinking about how you destroyed me. How could you pain me having your child growing in me? Once born, her eyes witnessed all, and you see; it was all because you couldn't be a fucking man, Oh wait! I take that back before you spit in my face again. Before you punch and squeeze my legs tight so that no one would notice. Grab me on my neck so that I couldn't scream and choke me. Hold me down so that I could not run, making me yell so that you found a reason to hit me. All because you fucked up. So, why does it feel like I am the wrong one? I remember how you'd smack me in the face when I came out of place. Looked me in the eyes and once again held my neck tight. I'd stay unconscious and wake up with you inside of me. Then you'd tell me it was all ok because you loved me. It was always my fault when you got with other women because I couldn't fuck you 5 to 6 times a day with your child growing inside of me. It was all my fault for staying longer than what I should have. It was all for the sake of my baby. I was afraid to leave and raise my children on my own. I wanted them to have what I never did. A father. That's all I ever wanted was to give them a fucking decent father. My heart was racing in fear and my head was pounding. This time I stood longer and yet again change was a broken promise. "If I see another BITCH, I swear I'll devour her." Fuck, what am I saying? You're already long gone, so why haven't I let go and said goodbye? You're implanted inside of me. Someone? I need saving, before I explode. "Don't fucking tell me to just let it go!" You hurt me. Fuck, just leave me alone. Stay out of my head, but you'll never physically go because I need you. I can never be alone. Sadly, it's time I turn to you. You. The razor who becomes my only friend. I turn to you for comfort. You take the pain away as you gently glide upon me. Now I sit alone and watch the beauty of my anguish leave my body. I keep turning to this because it's the

only thing that understands me enough to heal my
brokenness by breaking me physically somewhere else.
They say that physical pain is less than the mental pain
we endure. I believe that's true. I don't wanna relive
the pain of it all so i'll silence it with a blade
instead.

Sincerely,

Your friend, PTSD & Anxiety.

Chapter 4:
Night of terror

Why do I sit here and keep putting myself through this? Carson is so stuck on how I'm out for revenge, and how I'm out to make him pay for all the pain he's caused me, but I have no intentions to ever make him feel what I felt every single day that I was by his side. It was this feeling of helplessness, and choking, as if I couldn't breathe. This feeling of hysteria because he would tell me that I was delusional every day we fought. I started to believe him.

All of these thoughts crowded my mind as I began making my way towards the door to leave. I felt so alone when I had everyone who loved me surrounding me. The pain of dealing with women after women was tearing me apart. It never left my head all that he destroyed in me, but for some reason I always found a way to forgive him. I never saw myself loving him again, or ever being in a relationship; so, I guess that's why war began between us.

If I couldn't love him; he was sure to make my life a living hell. This man, an incredible father to my child, began haunting my life. Every time he'd begin with little white lies, and false promises of change. I would soften up a bit wanting to fix us for the sake of our baby. My parent's absence affected me. Imagine, it killed me to know my children were going down the same path.

I was sick of the same fucking routine, something had to change. I sought a psychiatric consultation. Later on they diagnosed me with Anxiety. Whenever I felt my anxiety overcoming me, or even when I felt too overwhelmed with a situation I couldn't confront at the moment, I'd take a walk. So, that's exactly what I did when my mother asked me to cool off that night.

It was 10pm. My mother at the time had these weird feelings about things so she told me to leave my jewelry. She insisted I shouldn't be walking around that late with jewelry on. I did what she asked, shrugged my shoulders, and laughed. I didn't really think much of it. So I walked a few blocks away from home, and felt a little relieved as tears ran across my cheeks. It was the middle of May, and you could feel summer approaching. I had this white oversized T-shirt on with some Eagle Ameri jeans, and my favorite Jean Chucks. I was not too far from my friend Joey's house so I decided to FaceTime him.

Joey, and I had somewhat of a history. In Junior High School, we were both kind of geeks, and funny looking. I somehow got out of that, and fell into the "Cool Kids" club, and Joey, well there wasn't much of a change for him. Everywhere I went I always kept an eye on my little Joey, and if any girl bothered him I was like the annoying big sister ready to attack.

After JHS we lost contact but faith brought us back together one day after over 10 years of being apart. We became the best of friends. This time appearances, and feelings changed. At least for me it did.

Joey was no longer geeky but handsome, and built. Things got weird between us now. I'd catch him looking at me longer and differently this time. I found myself calling him to hang out often. My mother loved him.

One day things heated up very quickly between us, we shared a kiss. Certain circumstances caused me to pull back, and I never really gave him the chance to win my heart. I guess I just didn't want to ruin our friendship if we didn't work out. Being friends was more important to me. I needed that friendly support. So, Joey was friend zoned as you can say.

Joey was always happy, and excited to hear from me, so when I called of course he wanted to spend some time catching up, and it was the perfect timing for me. I walked, and we carried a conversation over the phone. It was as if we never stopped talking, and naturally my feet led me towards his house. I told him I was so upset, and I needed someone to talk to. I needed to get away.

Joey was always available when I needed him the most. Of course, he stood on the phone with me while I vented. As I approached Joey's neighborhood our laughing over the phone continued. He always knew how to make me feel better with his stupid corny lines. I was so caught up in our conversation that I didn't even notice this hissing sound from behind me.

At the moment I figured it was some dumb ass young kid that was trying for my attention as I looked behind me. "Aye ma, you don't hear me calling you?" You can't be fucking serious. This kid was following me. He couldn't be more than 18 years old. I ignored him, and kept walking. Joey asked me if everything was ok, and if I needed him to come down.

I was always the type to put my pride up, and say "No I got this" and that's exactly what I did. I mean I was supposed to be Joey's Savior, not the other way around. This was our routine. I had no idea my life was in danger.

I started feeling a bit uneasy. The feeling of something bad was clouding my insides. Yet I ignored it once again as I walked faster. When I turned the corner towards Joey's building I looked back, and the kid was gone. I released a breath of air, and thanked God it wasn't something bad. I continued to walk towards Joey's courtyard, and then the front door. I slowed down thinking I was safe again. Suddenly I felt someone run up so fast behind me, I never even got the chance to turn around.

Joey was still on the phone with me when I told him I had arrived to buzz me in. Everything happened so quickly that I guess he figured I hung up on him. I could feel something against the lower right side of my back. It felt sharp and pinched against me. I wasn't sure what it was.

Then someone grabbed my hand where my phone was. "Keep walking, and don't fucking turn around yet". I stood in shock but for some reason my body did exactly what was told. I walked towards the elevator. "Turn around, and don't make noise" I slowly turned around and it was the kid again.

My heart was racing like a horse at the Kentucky derby. I could feel my face getting hot and heavy. My feet stood stuck in one spot. I couldn't move a muscle. I was in complete shock. I felt this intense knot in the pit of my stomach slowly creeping up and into my throat.

All I remember seeing was this huge knife swinging back and forth. I kept shouting that I had children and not to hurt me. He pulled up his shirt to show me a scar he blamed me for. This kid was fucking delusional or off of some type of drug. The kid couldn't even stand still which only made me more nervous. I told him I'd give him anything he wanted if he'd just let me go.

Then a miracle happened. Joey came running down the stairs and said "so, is this the reason you took forever?" He figured the guy was writing his phone number down on my phone or flirting with me, and he laughed. "Really Grace, i'm waiting on your little ass, and you tryna bag homeboy?" Somehow the kid managed to hide the knife behind himself in the process of Joey coming down the stairs. I looked at Joey with a serious, and worried face and it was as if my eyes spoke to him.

Everything turned serious and quiet in a matter of seconds. "Yo, you fucking with her?" Joey asked with this angry expression on his face. I bladed out quickly in fear "He took my phone Joey, he has a knife". Joey became uneased and slowly approached me. The kid told Joey to stay where he was as he came even closer to my body with the knife.

Somehow Joey distracted the kid by talking him down and back away from me. When the kid realized I started slowly moving, it was too late. I dashed to Joey running towards the stairs, as I looked back the kid ran out of the building. Joey grabbed my arm tightly, as we both ran upstairs to his house. I closed every lock behind me, ran to his room and shut the door tightly. This room became my sanctuary. I fell to my knees, and prayed to god as I thanked him. Joey held me tightly as tears poured down my face.

In an instant I blacked out, waking up in an Emergency Room. After all the stress; I had encountered a complete shutdown. Joey never left my side. The next morning my mother filed a police report. She couldn't stand to see the fear that ran across my face as I isolated myself from the world. It began haunting her.

I couldn't identify him in the police database of criminals in our area. I was still stuck in shock, and confusion. I wanted no part of this nightmare in finding him. I was afraid he'd retaliate and hurt my kids or family one day. Joey identified him in a line up. The police got to work and quickly caught him surrounding his building the next morning.

Apparently he robbed a thirteen year old with his nine year old sister who happened to reside in the same building as him. There were about five other people in that precinct that morning who made reports of a robbery by him. This kid was desperate. He robbed everyone he sought as an easy target.

The next day after we were put on stand to tell our encounters of that night. The Jury fell to tears as we watched the video recording of how I pleaded for my life by that elevator. His bail was set to half a million dollars, and even with him having to pay only 10% of it he still could not afford it. In my case alone he was given three years jail time, and five years probation. I felt he deserved more for taking away so much of me.

From that night on my whole world changed. I couldn't sleep at night, I'd wake up pouring in sweat, screaming and fighting. Everywhere I went it had to be before night and even in daylight I had all eyes watching every corner, walking alongside someone. I questioned everyone's motives and never spoke much of what happened again. At times, I still catch myself drifting off, and seeing his face still.

    I dreaded the day of his release. I couldn't imagine sharing a world with the same man who took so much of it from me, the man who almost took my life and almost left my children motherless for the rest of their lives. And all for what? A damn phone and money. What kind of monster would he be in 3 years from now? I may never know the answers and that terrifies me the most.

**Chapter 5:
Black Wave**

So we're taking a step back into the past a little. Before my mother left to start her new life in Florida; after Carson broke me down, and left. This is the story of a boy who had me in lust, and invaded my mind for a while. A boy who completely used me. Who told me I wasn't enough for him because I had kids and no job.

It started off as any other normal boring day in my life. The first time I even noticed Stephon. I was minding my business, and carrying on a conversation with an old friend. Stephon came out of a building next to mine one day shirtless. This was our first time even meeting. I never paid attention to him before.

Stephon approached me and made a silly joke when he saw me. He stared at me, and smiled as he got back into his car and it caught my interest as he drove off. For days I remained curious, so it began. Stephon's mischievous smirk lingered all over me. It was impossible not to lust over him.

I would go outside more often than usual just to bump into him. I would even go on store runs every time my mom needed something. I began this routine, and even got used to the songs he played from his car outside my window. At that point I already knew when he was around. One day I got the courage to meet him outside, and actually speak to him.

What the fuck did i just get myself into? That day Stephon got my number and the adventure began. We were so damn careless of what was to come. We would text as if we were teenagers in high school. Night after night. Stephon would check on me throughout the day. I had butterflies in my stomach. It was cute.

Stephon had me so sprung not only by his words but also by his voice. We shared a passion, and dream for music. I began downloading, and listening to his music over, and over again until I memorized each, and every lyric. I wanted Stephon, and I didn't care for anyone's opinions. One day we let go, and gave in.

Stephon invited me to stay the night with him. We talked for a bit when I arrived. Then the fun began as he kissed me and undressed me. It was a rush finally getting that feeling of lust I had for him out. Every time he texted me after that we'd link up and spend our day or night in euphoria.

We weren't aware of the decision we made to not be safe would later on cost a life. Although Stephon thought he was careful, and pulled out in time it was already too late. That choice we made put a strain on our communication. Stephon knew what he'd done yet wanted no part of the consequences that emerged from not using our fucking brains.

After that night we went weeks without speaking. Days soon turned into weeks. My mornings now started off with dizziness, and throwing up. I was weak, and afraid.

Then eventually I missed my period. An HCG test confirmed my fear. I was pregnant.

For days my calls were sent to voicemail, and I had no contact with Stephon. Another fatherless child. Then one day I finally got through to him from a friend, and invited him over for dinner. Surprisingly he agreed to meet me. At that point I was fed up with the distance between us, and disappointed in him. So I got right to the point, and told him I was pregnant during dinner.

Figures. Stephon gave me every reason why I could not have this child. Not one damn reason mattered. For days I was angry, and confused but most of all in pain. Day after day of stress. My hormone levels were dropping, and fast. One night the pain became unbearable and I rushed to the emergency room. It was the most heartbreaking night of my life.

They say that everything happens for a reason, but what the fuck could possibly be the reason for this?

Doctor's told me I needed a lot of bed rest. Baby love had a chance at survival. So I did exactly what was told. Unfortunately it wasn't enough. The next day I returned to the emergency room. I was given meds to help the pain, and help ease the labor. Then I was sent back home. I had to prepare myself for a night that I would never forget.

That night I got up from bed, and walked to my kitchen for some water. The next thing I remember was waking up on my kitchen floor with my mom screaming and crying; trying to fully wake me up. I had no idea what had happened, and my head was pounding. I was wet, and cold.

My Mom, and stepdad called an ambulance. I was weak, and tired. I could barely see what was going on. As I lifted my hands all I could see was blood everywhere. My heart sank, and my eyes shut once more. I was losing so much blood, and fast. I woke up again in an ambulance connected to IV lines pouring from both of

my arms. I had fainted twice in one night. I remember
waking up for the last time in a hospital bed.

My mom was nervous, still crying, and signing
papers to authorize for a blood transfusion. "God,
please give me the strength to get up. Help me fight
this. Don't let me die."
These words kept replaying inside of my head as I
watched my mother fall apart. Suddenly what felt like a
miracle happened. My vital signs were coming back up,
and the paleness in my face became more life like again.
A doctor came in, and had so much pain in her eyes as
she told me I was losing my baby.

The worst part was having to give one more push to
get what was left inside of me out. Every inch of my
body trembled as I pushed with what little strength I
had left in me, and I completely broke down. This child
had no chance of a beautiful life because of me. I began
beating myself up over it. Blaming myself everyday.

Maybe if I didn't stress so much my angel would have had a chance.

The whole time this was happening Stephon was nowhere to be found. My heart was full of anger, and pain. Once again weeks past. Stephon finally texted me. I wanted to ignore him so badly but I also wanted some closure, and answers as to why he abandoned us in such a way. As he gave me excuses I only grew more resentment towards him until I let him go.

Overtime I finally learned to forgive myself, and saw why it wasn't gonna last with us. I saw why my angel didn't survive. Stephon was slowly wasting his life away in these streets, and hanging around the wrong people. Stephon didn't deserve my love nor my child's. We deserved better. Stephon would never have been a good father.

Chapter 5.5:

Loss- battle #2

"What just happened? My mom, why is she crying? Ugh, my head is pounding. What's going on? you fainted."
There's blood on the floor, and your hands. I know what is happening here. I just can't comprehend it all. Am I dying?

"God, please give me strength, don't let me die."
There's IV lines on both my arms. This can't be good.
Just breathe Grace.

"Mom, I'm so scared." She looks at me with this brave face but I know inside she's afraid, as much as I am.

The doctors are scrambling, and trying to figure out if I need a transfusion or not.
The whole damn time I've been wondering where the hell Stephon is. Why hasn't he answered my mom's phone calls? Where the fuck is that asshole?

Then a Nurse comes in, and cleans the blood leaking from my thighs.

I have to push my child out now. "God, please give me strength." "One big push Grace" I'm not ready. I push and see this ball of blood. It was as if time stood still and I was stuck in the twilight zone.

They move me from one bed to another, and inject my line with some pain medication.

Stephon took my heart, and stole the life from inside of me. I feel dead, yet I'm still alive enduring this torture.

I'm weak. I need to see a light in this darkness that shadows me. I'm falling off the deep end. Mom tells me that with time the pain will heal.

She tells me to look forward to tomorrow because today didn't have to determine what my future would be like. So for today i would bask in my pain, and tomorrow it will lessen.

Tomorrow approaches. I still feel like shit.

But at least I'm alive.

No, fuck this i dont want to be here. I hope this bastard gets what he deserves. I hope he is tormented by the tiny face that could have been ours.

"I can't breath"

                    Sincerely,

                        your friend Anxiety.

Chapter 6:

Exchange

Fast forward to my life in florida..

After two hours of this online safety drivers course I was exhausted and hungry sitting in this library. My step sister and I decided to take a break from the world of literature, and grab some food. It was our first time being in this area, so we walked about two streets down and crossed a railroad. Naturally I leaned towards a coffee shop but my little sister was more of a chilled spot, and I didn't mind.

We decided on a restaurant. I remember walking in and seeing this menu on a huge flat screen television. I couldn't decide what I wanted, then this man answered us, and for some reason at that moment my heart felt as if it skipped a beat. I have this flaw that with the attention of a bad boy I turn real pendeja and submissive to anything they ask of me. It's fucking ridiculous.

We carried on with a small conversation and I could already see where this was going. I felt this sudden attraction towards him. I guess you could call it; lust at first sight. He was born and raised in the South Bronx, and he had everything I desire in a man.

I could already feel the adrenaline and all we had exchanged were a few sentences. We ended our conversation with him offering me a position at his restaurant and of course, I accepted his offer. I took his name and number on his business card, and continued on my way. My little sister chuckled the whole way back home, stating the obvious. This man was now the new owner to my thoughts and time.

About two weeks went by, and I studied my ass off for this permit exam, in which I finally passed. My mother's boyfriend at the time took me for a drive, and it was the first day I drove on my own. How amazing was it to be roaming freely on the streets of Florida, where the summer heat beamed from the mirrors, and the winds blew upon my face. I was so excited.

That same day I decided to go back to the restaurant in hopes that I'd run into my new savior. Unfortunately, he wasn't around but everyone knew who I was already. I explained how sorry I was for not calling before but somewhere along my trip back home I lost the business card. Reign, an employee of the restaurant, explained that I could come back the next morning for my interview.

It couldn't come any faster. That night it felt a little more difficult to fall asleep. I was tossing and turning all night. It must've been the excitement of a new job, and new friends. I had a chance of finally starting over in a new state or probably just the feeling Joe gave me.

The next morning, I awoke to my children's screams. My alarm clock every morning. I got ready and headed on my way downtown. It was my first time using the busing schedule down south. There was only one bus that passed by, and only by the hour. I felt excited to be traveling in a new city.

I arrived at the restaurant about 10 minutes after my scheduled time. Shit, great first impression. I explained to my new boss Joe that the bus scheduling sucked in florida. It was my first time traveling in Florida on my own. I had to find my way around. Joe just chuckled and found it cute how apologetic I was.

I started training for a few days. Everyday Joe would have a coworker drive me home until it became a constant routine. Then came a day in which Joe and I were the only ones working after Lunch rush. I couldn't stop smiling at him. Every time he'd look my way I'd try so hard to keep my cool. We began joking around, talking, and hanging out more every day.

Joe would pick me up, and drop me back home after work. The days the restaurant was slow he'd take me to the office to work. Joe knew how happy it made me just to be occupied with him every day. Keeping busy made the stress New York had on me. Florida was definitely the perfect escape.

I loved every moment I spent with Joe. He was the only man who wanted to do so much for me in every aspect. Joe challenged me to step outside of my comfort zone and encouraged me to strive for more in life. He showed me that I'm much more than just a statistic, and more than an average girl. He gave me motivation.

Joe's passion for what he loved, and his strive for success was incredible to me. Not only did I fall for him, but I fell for his hustle too. It's funny how a stranger can have such a huge impact in your life, and support you more than the people who constantly surround you. Joe was a hard dedicated working man. Everything I needed in someone.

I remember the day everything changed between us. It was the beginning of July. A hot summer day just like every other day down south. My birthday was approaching. Joe offered to give me a ride to go shopping. We had planned a social outing, but as always something got in the way.

Later that night, I called Joe and cancelled. I thought my birthday would be spent stuck at home bored, and alone. Joe had other plans in mind. The next day Joe invited me over to his place for dinner, and drinks.

I'm a city girl used to living in an apartment building. Listening to rap, hiphop, and spanish music playing at 2am from outside of my window. Seeing mice run past you from garbage bags dumped on the streets. This was normal for a New yorker.

When I arrived at Joe's place I was astonished. It was huge, and seemed like a mansion to me. He really must've worked hard to build such a beautiful empire. I was amazed as he led me through the door, and into the kitchen. We had an amazing dinner and talked for about two hours. It felt good to just forget about my troubles and just laugh for one night.

Somehow in the midst of dinner we ended up walking into the living room, and up the stairs to his bedroom. The bed must've taken up half of his room, and his room was huge. It had a personal bathroom, and even a walk-in closet. I was truly in love as it looked exactly like how I would want my dream home to be.

As the drinks kept pouring I could feel myself getting drunk. It was my birthday celebration dinner so I didn't care how much I had to drink. I was happy, and giggly the whole time. I started dancing to some music Joe played on his stereo. Eventually I bumped into his nightstand spilling my drink all over me. It was like a scene straight from a movie. We couldn't stop laughing.

Joe offered me one of his shirts. As I changed into it I could feel him watching me. I smirked, and approached him to dance some more. I could feel the room slowly spinning, and that was my hint to stop drinking.

Joe laid me down onto his bed, and laughed at how drunk I was.

I couldn't help but smile as he told me how cute I looked being drunk, and happy. I remember moving away from him only because my heart wouldn't stop racing. I knew what was coming while I laid in nothing but his black T-shirt. Joe followed behind me then pulled me closer to him. I could feel his body shaking, and I'm sure he felt mine as he held me tightly.

I let myself drift into the moment and it felt so perfect. Joe gently grabbed my face and kissed me. I felt his hands caressing my body, and my breathing became even deeper as my body weakened. Joe began kissing on my neck as I grabbed him to lay on me. I wrapped my right leg around his body as he took off my shirt. Joe began kissing all around my collarbone then onto my breast.

Joe's tongue slowly rotated around my nipples as he gently massaged my curves lowering down to my thong. In a matter of seconds my thong was down to my knees, and his face in between my legs. I don't know about you, but for me everything feels more intense when I'm drinking. I didn't want it to stop. I had this euphoric feeling.

Joe continued licking my thighs until he completely removed my thong. He elevated towards me rather than inside of me. I could see in his face how he longed for this moment. Joe removed his jeans, strapped up, and slowly entered me. The passionate kissing got more, and more intense with each stroke. Finally, we both reached climax after about 10 minutes of hot passionate sex.

This night was an incredible, and unforgettable one. Joe already had me in the palm of his hands. He had no idea what would happen in the weeks ahead. It truly became depressing.

We continued our hidden romance in the days ahead, and it only became even more intense. I was his rider, and he was my stallion. A prince charming you can say.

My feelings began growing stronger but things at home were only worsening.

I was now living in a strict environment. I couldn't stay out past 8pm. I couldn't have friends over. I wasn't allowed to have any type of alcoholic drinks. I started missing days of work because I no longer had my mothers support with my kids.

Once again my mother bagan letting another man dictate her actions. It was as if her new boyfriend didn't like that she was giving all her time to me now. He hated that my mother even had her own source of income from babysitting while I worked. He was envious that my mother had someone spending funds on her, and not on him.

One day I opened up about what was going on at home to Joe. That's when everything began to change between us. He felt that he was at fault for the dysfunction going on. Joe wanted nothing but the best for me, and he didn't want to be a part of me getting kicked out.

It felt as if my dreams were crushed for a moment. I lost my job, and a connection I had with someone who lessened my stressors. Joe eventually became distant. Once again another wasted romance. I was left on Read, and Seen in every message I sent to him. My calls were suddenly forwarded to voicemail. What the fuck do I do?

For some reason, Joe sensed I wanted out of this misery I was living. The only reason I stood was for him. So just like that, something that began so beautifully ended in another heartbreak. The resentment from losing everything that was making me happy again started emerging. I eventually got kicked out.

The most amazing part of that experience was the memories he left me. The memories of riding beside him through his hustle. Listening to his favorite song as we drove through the sunshine state. Watching him work, and being a part of his work. Every day I spent with him was a great day.

Even laying beside him, and holding him close as he fell asleep made me smile. Going out for lunch, and drinks while we talked of future goals, and dreams were my favorite memories. Although it was for a short amount of time, Joe made my life feel a bit at ease. For that I'll forever be grateful.

I try to understand that at times people are put in our lives temporarily. Sometimes to lessen the pain we are going through at the moment. I never learned to say goodbye when it was time to let someone go. I thank Lost Man for that. The man always left without saying goodbye so I never got closure. I kept holding on.

I mean honestly speaking, how do you even let go of something that once made up so much of your happiness? Only to go back to such sorrow, and misery. How do you explain to your mind, and heart that you will never see, or share another moment with someone again. Goodbye life in Florida. Goodbye Joe. Goodbye Horses.

Chapter 6.5:

Blackout- Battle #3

Have you ever felt so stuck in your life?
Have you ever felt as if you will never go any further?
Every day I wake up questioning myself.
what the fuck am I doing?
Am I even a good enough mother, Daughter, Sister, Or Friend?
Am I a good enough writer?
I know I don't live life by the rules that we're supposed to be living by.
How do we really know what the fuck the rules are?
There's no instructions on how to live.
No one tells you that life is shit as a child.
You just experience it on your own.
I wanna do all these incredible things but the moment I try to change everyone is already criticizing me, and judging my motives.

Of course, we can't change from one day to the next when
we are so accustomed to living a certain way.
We fear change.
Which is totally sad to say because we should only fear
the judgment of God if we are living a sinful life
aren't we?
How do I stop feeling like a failure?
You would think it's something so simple to stop.
But it isn't.
I could go back to therapy, but who the fuck are they to
say what I'm suppose to feel or not feel?
I don't need someone to analyze that as a child I was
physically abused.
As a child I was sexually molested.
As a child I witnessed domestic violence that continued
on into my life.
I don't need someone analyzing that I have Daddy fucking
issues.
Let's be honest.

What the fuck are they really gonna do besides pop pills into you, and tell you to practice your grounding techniques in the middle of a fucking blackout.

I'm fucked up.

I could give you a million reasons why, and there will always be a "But" or questions behind every solution.

There's always a fucking "But" involved.

That's called Anxiety.

I've asked myself as a god fearing woman because I was raised to never question god's motives, but I am curious.

Why is this life made of tests?

Why are we constantly challenged?

God, why me?

I remember moving to Florida, and just thinking how lucky I was to be starting a new life.

I had a new opportunity at providing the right life for my kids.

I began a new job, and even joined a church.

I mean at first I didn't feel right being there, and my heart wasn't fully committed.

But after a while of going it started to feel right.

I still sinned but not as much.

I'm not perfect.

I'm learning.

I could feel myself changing.

I finally felt happy in my life.

Everything was going right.

I guess like every other thing in life that has a beginning, there's an ending as well.

I gave in, and gave up.

Not on god but on love, and family.

If I am to be judged so much for my past, why should I keep trying?

I felt like being a Christian for everyone else besides myself was bringing me down.

I guess I gave up on faith.

Why would he work on me?

Why would he bless me, and change my life?

He's already given up on me.

I'm a waste.

All of these unanswered questions?

But that's how the devil works right?

Using my anxiety, depression, and post traumatic stress to pull me away.

I know this.

Yet I still fall weak.

Why are there so many restrictions?

Most of these things I wanted to do in life didn't involve sinning.

Now I had to completely change who I was because people said so.

I had to wear a skirt because people said so.

I had to cover my tattoos because it wasn't appealing to people.

Who the fuck are you?

I don't want a relationship with you.

I want it with God.

You can't tell me why I feel worthless.

You can't make this pain go away.

I'm so tired of being judged.

Yes, I make mistakes.

Yes, I still get angry.

Yes, I still sin.

But you're not God.

So please, leave me be.

No one is perfect.

I want to change, and do it the way I feel is most comfortable, and right.

In time I'll get it right.

God please help me out of this feeling.

I just want to be happy. I just want to be loved.

Why am I not enough?

Sincerely,

Your Friend Anxiety.

Chapter 7:

H.I.M

Back to New York.

I decided that moving in with Seth would be the best option. I mean I wasn't gonna stay stranded in Florida with nowhere else to go. So, we rode the train back to the city that never sleeps. 26 hours later. You could feel the change in the atmosphere. It was no longer sunny.

The city was making me weep. well at least the Bronx was. I hated living here. The constant fights, arguing, and shoot outs at all types of time in the day, or night. The bullshit drama one had to endure at work, or even walking to the corner store.

So, here's a little history behind this chapter. I was free, and a wild spirited girl who loved living in the night life. Parties, Clubs, lounges, and bars. Drinking, and dancing was my escape from reality. It was a life in which I could meet new people, and didn't have to worry about remembering their names because the next day I was gone. So to say it was as if I was living a double life, and I lusted for it.

I started College again. Joined a music club. Sang my ass off, and loved every moment of it. Music became my escape. In the midst of classes I met Cash. Cash was another free, and wild spirited girl. We clicked, and started hanging out more, and more.

I lasted about a month in Seth's place. It wasn't long before he kicked me out because I wouldn't fuck him. Seth thought he would use me for sex because he took us in. I'd rather be homeless than to open that dysfunctional door again. So, back to the shelter intake center.

This time we got denied for leaving the first time. They figured we had somewhere to stay. I was over the bullshit games these fucking people were playing. I must've called about three different family members, and friends. All gave me excuses as to why we couldn't stay with them. Then finally, one family member agreed to let us stay with them.

I was relieved. The apartment was closer to my college, and there was a great school for the kids. There was even a daycare in the building for Violet-Ann. I managed to go to school part-time, and work. Everything was falling into place. My grades were looking amazing. GPA of 3.7, and money in my pocket. I'd progress in no time.

Once Midterms, and finals were over I'd go out, and celebrate with Cash. One night I met a guy at this bar Cash took me to. Lucas was his name. We had fun for a while.

Lucas would drive me around from time to time, and we'd talk. We went on movie dates, and hung out. Of course we got intimate here, and there. Lucas was really someone I used to pass the time. There was really no future for us.

We kept having more nights to forget over, and over again. It was boring. Lucas was a nice, helpful, and sweet guy. But a liar. Lucas wanted more than just a friendship, or relationship. Lucas wanted a marriage. Lucas wanted his fucking green card.

I guess I wasn't the only one using him. Lucas had a girlfriend in another country, and was here on a work visa. That wasn't the worst part. Lucas had another girl who contacted me saying they were together. I guess that's why I couldn't see a future with him. I ended this fling, and moved on. Good riddance.

I decided to give boys a break, and focus on school. It was just a fucking headache trying to find the right relationship. Months passed, and I was enjoying being alone. No one spilling insecurities, or past traumas on me. I was at peace. They say that love tends to creep up on you when you least expect it.

December 9th of 2016. It was a chilly but calm night. I decided to head out for some drinks. You meet a lot of people when you're living the social nightlife. I called up a few friends, and we all linked up at a lounge.

My friend Sara wanted to introduce me to some of her friends. Matthew was one of them. I'd seen him before but I never gave thought to where I'd seen him. Matthew had this sweet smile, and was attractive. My head said "Grace, don't you dare start again."

Matthew kept looking at me, and finally pulled me out to dance. "Here we go again." I danced most of the night with him as we laughed, and drank. I couldn't stop grinning. I knew I was drunk already. We decided to leave as the lounge was getting dull.

Matthew insisted on walking Sara, and I home. As I walked I could feel the temperature dropping. Matthew noticed I was cold. Of course, he was the perfect gentleman. Matthew offered me his jacket.

We finally arrived at our location, and I could see that Matthew looked as if he was waiting for something more. I said goodnight, and went upstairs. Sounds boring doesn't it? Trust me this story gets better.

I continued on as if nothing happened for the next few days to come. I guess Matthew found me through Sara's social media, and sent me a follow. Talk about persistence. I wasn't really interested in continuing anything more than that dance we shared. Matthew kept writing to me until I finally responded.

A few weeks passed, and Sara invited me to another party. Of course I agreed to attend. Matthew reached out and was interested in seeing me again. So we met up again at Sara's friend's party. Tus the start of another disaster.

I could tell Matthew was already in love with me. A friend of his tried approaching me to dance, and he got super defensive over it. He stated to his friend that I was his girl, and that he needed to back off. Normally, I would've said hell no but for some reason I liked the sound of that coming from Matthew. I ignored the shit out of that red flag.

As the night was ending, and I was getting ready to go home Matthew asked to speak with me in the hallway. Matthew figured it was the right time to make a move. Of course my girls at that exact moment came out of the apartment, and caught it all. Matthew, and I had our own High School makeout session, and our cheerleaders cheered us on.

We agreed to go back to Matthew's place. In the midst of the party it began snowing. Both drunk, we started a snowball fight outside, and kissed again. It was like a fucking scene straight out of a movie. Finally we made it to his place.

We couldn't stop laughing as we walked through the hallway to his bedroom. Everything became silent as Matthew whispered to stay quiet. His mother was in the next room fast asleep. Red flag number two.

Matthew gave me something more comfortable to change into as he showered. I anxiously waited. His room was kept up well so I could tell he was an organized person. He finally finished in the shower, and we got right into business. Another night of pleasure from a stranger I had no care or tie too.

The next day he reached out to me again, and I ignored him. I wasn't emotionally available. Relationships were fucking drainging, and a shit show. Loneliness can be a bitch if I'm being honest. If you're like me with abandonment issues you tend to settle for anything so that you're not alone.

Matthew eventually reached out to Sara, and as a friend she encouraged me to give him a try. Sara felt it was time that I gave love another try. So that's what I did. I gave Matthew a chance. We began dating. It was actually amazing. He took me out on dates every weekend, and spoiled me with cute gifts. He really knew how to make a girl smile.

Every moment I spent with him felt like magic, and each day I wanted to see him more. Just being around him made me happy. He was fun, and that's what I enjoyed about him the most. I could see the excitement in his eyes, and the glow he had every time he saw me. It was truly a fucking fairytale come to life.

A month later he confirmed it. Matthew said he loved me. Red flag number 3. I was ignoring all of the signs of a toxic relationship that was slowly unfolding. With all that I had gone through with Seth, and Carson I was reluctant to love again. I was afraid. I mean can you really blame me. Look at all the bullshit I've dealt with so far.

A few months flew by, and I found myself eventually feeling the same. I'd fallen in love with Matthew, and I felt comfortable with telling him at this point. Why is it once we become vulnerable, and finally let down our guard shit starts messing up. It's like the universe turns against you.

Things began to change. As I began investing more time, love, and effort into Matthew he was giving his elsewhere. I found that we were arguing more often than usual. We argued about the smallest thing one evening, and Matthew decided to break it off with me.

I was left in confusion. I couldn't understand how someone who loved you could just up, and leave you with no real explanation. I couldn't comprehend it. You don't just wake up one morning, and say "Hey, I don't love you anymore." There was more to the story, and I wanted to know why. We were just literally happy.

Matthew broke up with me through a damn fucking text message. He didn't even have the balls to face me in person. Fucking coward. He kept saying how he still loved me, and how it was hurting him to break up with me. I was torn yet I only became full of anger. How dare he say he still loved me?

Days passed, and I felt more Frustrated. I decided to finally let go after a week of unanswered questions.

Then Matthew called me stating he wanted to talk. I agreed to meet up at a park close to me.

Matthew explained how he regretted leaving me, and how confused he felt. He stated the relationship was new, and complicated for him being that I already had three children. Mind you he had a kid of his own so I knew that was bullshit.

I explained to Matthew that good things in life are worth having but it wouldn't be easy. We have to fight for it but in the end the outcome is truly amazing. That's how love works for me. If he continued running away he'd never find happiness. I still loved him so of course I agreed to fix things with him when he asked to start over.

That same day as we sat in the park I got a message over social media, and I was in complete shock. It was Matthew's ex-girlfriend asking if him, and I were in a relationship. Apparently he was in a relationship with her way before me, and they were still together. I bet you didn't see that coming. Neither did I.

Now I was the other woman. The past week he left me he visited her, and they hooked up. I should've seen the signs. He really broke up with me to be with her. Of course he came running back to me because I mean look at me. I'm fucking awesome. Right? Wrong. If I was so awesome none of this shit would keep happening to me.

For that moment my heart felt as if it had dropped to the floor, and everything around me was spinning. I was stuck in shock. My stomach was just turning the whole time he tried apologizing. Excuses after excuses came pouring from that man's mouth.

How the fuck did I not notice this? I was with him damn near every day. How the fuck do you carry on with someone knowing you belong to another? He kept explaining how he never ended it because they lived in different states. Yet almost every other weekend he was with her while he said he was visiting his family. I even visited his family with him a few times before so I couldn't understand shit.

Matthew begged, and pleaded to me how he never cheated because we were separated. That was a load of bullshit. His ex proved different. She had calls records he made to her, and text messages stating how he loved her over the time period of our relationship. Matthew even wore a sweater I gifted him to go see her. She sent me a photo of him holding her child wearing that same sweater.

I was so blinded by love you can imagine what happened next. Yep, I forgave him, and continued in a relationship with him. Months passed, and it still ate me up inside so the arguments continued. The image of her touching his body began to haunt me. Everything he did was questioned.

I wanted nothing but to try and fix us. So I made a promise to let it go, and move forward for my peace. I paid less attention to what Matthew did and focused on school again. Plus I had an old friend reaching out to me to keep busy. Paris. No guys, nothing happens with him and I. The kid was behind bars. Paris was someone who helped me pass the time. A good friend.

Things were getting better between Matthew and I. I wasn't bothered by the past anymore. We finally decided to move in together at the "Lost Man's" place. I lost contact with Paris and began focusing on Matthew again.

Boy was that a mistake. The fights started again, and this time stronger. It was our environment causing stress. Just living somewhere I felt unwanted had me on edge. I started pouring it onto Matthew as he had no job, and was depending on me to get by.

Plus the long distance relationship I had with the "Lost Man" wasn't helping ease the stress. It felt weird living under his roof when he disappeared from me as a child. It was just a shitty situation all around. Living in a mess, and constantly picking up after everyone there. They were nothing like how my old home was with my mother. It was honestly depressing.

Matthew, and I decided to make a desperate move. We got married, and left. We hopped from hotel's to Motel's, and finally into a shelter to start our new life together. I was willing to make a sacrifice for the sake of my kids' stability. A mother's love is like no other.

I wanted a home for my kids. They needed a home. I owed them at least that much. I married for stability, and that's one of the worst things to do. That's in my opinion.

Back into the intake center we went. This time the process was quicker. I had the help of someone else by my side. Matthew was willing to face anything that came our way as long as he was doing it beside me. That right there made life a bit easier. Knowing I finally had someone in my corner.

We were given a placement in a family shelter. It was a small one-bedroom but it was now our home. The heat wasn't great, and the beds were hard as fuck but I was grateful to have a roof over our heads. I wouldn't have to worry about a place to rest our heads anymore. No more hotels. No more long nights laying awake on a bench so that my kids could rest.

Life in the shelter started off ruff. We had no money, no jobs, and no food. It was a process of applying for public assistance to have a few dollars, and food to get us by until we could work. I remember asking my mother for money, and using about 30 dollars in a dollar store on a small pot, paper plates, cups, and spoons. A small bag of rice, a small oil, a pack of the cheapest chicken in there.

I stretched that food out for about 3 days; along with the extra snack baggies I grabbed from the intake center. Then on the third day when we were running out of food I remember going into a restaurant desperate. It was the first time I found myself begging for food. Thankfully the owner was a good man, and he gave us more than what I asked for. We had a meal for another 3 days.

By that time I had found a source of income, and we were finally getting back on track. Life got a bit easier. My kids were in a good school and my husband found work. Shortly after I began work. We were happy again, and living great despite the environment.

Three month's into our marriage it all changed. For whatever reason I thought we were past all the pain we caused one another being married. Marriage is literally just a piece of paper that doesn't change who a person is. I believe that a marriage without God is no marriage at all. We didn't have faith.

Instead of the two of us there were now three of us involved in this marriage. Matthew let himself go to another stranger. A one nighter that later on brought upon my pain, and even more damage. He kept this a secret for another three months after, and the pain worsened inside of me.

Matthew had unprotected sex with a girl from work. I knew something was wrong when he arrived home at 10am the next morning, wasted and smelling of liquor. My heart literally felt like it dropped into my stomach. I couldn't believe it really happened again. This time in our marriage.

How could he be so damn careless? I was sick. The most embarrassing part was having to explain to a doctor how I got sick. Then having a damn needle the size of hell stuck into my asscheek. I tried pretending as if I were ok for the sake of our marriage. It meant everything to me, and my husband did too.

I swore on a bible to love him through thick and thin. Until death did us apart. With all that pain I once again set it aside, and told him we would get through it. My marriage meant more to me than divorce. Unfortunately he didn't feel the same.

Something changed inside of him. He was no longer the man I fell in love with. Matthew wanted a divorce, and he didn't want anything to do with me. Once again I was left in the dark. The crazy coincidence is that a year ago that same month is when he cheated the first time. I was convinced that something was clearly wrong.

Matthew came home one night, and we were already arguing via text. It sounded as if he was just desperate to leave at this point. Finding any reason to fight. As if I were the cause of his blackouts, and the reason as to why he felt so suffocated. Maybe I was.

I begged and pleaded for him to stay home but I guess our love wasn't strong enough. I blocked the door and cried as he forcefully made his way out. Eventually he got me to move and he ran off. All of my emotions surfaced, and the thought of being alone in that shelter scared the shit out of me. So, I ran after him and into the dark rainy night.

I called out his name as I fell to my knees but he was gone. I felt weak and it felt as if my life just ended. Everything I worked hard for slipped right out of my hands. I had no idea what the fuck just happened. I failed as a wife.

The days after were the worst ones yet. I had fallen into a depression. For about a week I couldn't get out of bed. My neighbor was aware of what had taken place, and decided to help me through it. Everyday she would come over, and cook for all of us. I didn't see myself getting out of the depression. Eventually I did.

Chapter 7.5:

solitude- battle #4

Night 3 and I still haven't fallen asleep. It's 6am. I must've slept for about an hour or so because today I saw him. He passed my kitchen, and I screamed for his name. "Matthew" I searched the whole house in hopes of finding him but of course it was just my mind playing tricks on me. It's night again and this time I spray his cologne all over my sheets and pillows. Another night I cry myself to sleep wondering when will he return home to his family. His cologne made my heart beat faster and the memories of the nights we slept together suddenly overcame me. I can't fucking sleep all I see is his face surrounding me. When he left, he had no idea how much of me he took with him.

God when will he return home? I can't eat. I can't sleep. I can't do anything. How the fuck did we get to this point? I loved him. I tried everything in my power

to love him, and be the best wife I could possibly be.
Please come home.

I don't know how much longer I can take this. Maybe if I
call his job he'll answer me. He's not even at work. So
where could he be? Is he with another woman? Why can't
he just come home? God please. I can't lose my marriage.
"The number you have dialed is no longer in service" Is
it because of my 32 voice messages? I know it is. He
changed his number, but we're still married. God please,
why is he doing this to me? It's been a week, and I
still haven't heard from him.

God please, I'm losing it. I need you..

He's never coming back home is he? How will I continue
on? I know you all are saying how pathetic right? "NO!
no, one is saying Grace". You're in love. This is a
marriage so you fight. Don't give up, he will return
home. Have faith. No!

It's over. He abandoned me. Now I have to start all over
again. Fuck!

What happened to our promises? Through thick and fucking thin MATTHEW! Why? God, I'm drowning. Now I'm alone.

Sincerely,

Your friend Anxiety, & Depression.

Chapter 8:

Changes

Matthew was gone.

Something had to give already. I was losing myself. If Matthew did not return I'd have to be moved into another shelter. We were almost close to getting our apartment. Literally two months away to be exact.

I woke up when social services visited me. I was so deep into my depression that I couldn't get up to take my kids to school for that week. I was forced back into therapy, and on medication. It helped me to stop feeling or even caring anymore.

Just as I began moving forward, Matthew appeared. This time I was different. I agreed to let him come back since my leasing signing was coming up. When Matthew came home I finally found the reason he really left, and wanted a divorce. He was with his ex-girlfriend again.

So, that day I decided to meet up with Sara, and that is when I met Rob. Rob was the man that would make me forget about Matthew, and brought me peace again. Rob was different. He didn't like the social nightlife. He was older, and had his shit together. Rob understood me, and it wasn't complicated. He loved me for me. Flaws, and all.

Everything changed. I was now spending my weekends with Rob. I was able to just sing while we drove around, and he'd just laugh. He didn't judge me. Rob's love was like no other love I've felt. I could be honest with him without fear. Even with our small arguments he'd grab me, kiss me, and make me forget what I was upset about.

Our intimacy was even at its best. There was no pain. Even when I'd start falling into my isolation, and depression, Rob lifted me, and gave me motivation. He made everything feel as if it would be ok and I was now safe. Rob was everything I needed.

Chapter 8.5:

Young girl, don't cry- battle #5

(Backtracking to when I lived with Matthew, before Rob came along.)

Some days I wake up perfectly normal and ready to go. Those are the days I long for the most. The days in which I didn't miss a thing. The days in which I made the right choices. Don't we all? Other days I wake up in complete silence and emptiness. I believe that I am alone and that the world has nothing to offer. For that day, I am lost. I am no one, and no one is me. How can you possibly understand me, if you aren't me? You don't know how a certain action will cause my reaction. So, let me try to explain it in a way that would help me understand it, so that you may understand, if you get what I mean.

There are objects in our lives that are called triggers. These triggers can unleash a bullet so fierce that literally can explode on whatever it hits.

I'm smiling and laughing with him. Having the best time. Then he says he must go. He grabs the same sweater he wore in the photo when he was with her. The same sweater he had on when he sat on her sofa holding her child. The same morning he told me he was at work.

Sweater = Trigger.

I don't mean to think this way but I do. I wish it could stop. Now the feeling of when I found out creeps on me. Some may say, get rid of the sweater. It's more to the story than just that. Some may say that it's my fault for accepting this type of relationship. You see, that's the thing with PTSD. It creeps up behind you when you least expect it. The images stay carved into your brain.

Events begin to replay over and over again. It's like a fucking twilight zone. I can tell myself I forgive him. Let's just forget it never happened. Then this demon that haunts me. It tends to fill my head with lies. Lies that I will be ok and then when I am, it comes back three times worse to devour my happiness.

Fear then starts to kick in. I can't sleep at night because I'm tossing and turning. Thinking about what you did. It's destroying me. In my lonely hour the questions emerge. Will anyone ever want me with three kids? Or yet will anyone I want, want me back?

I thought I found him. Someone who caused me such heartbreak, yet is learning himself how to love. You see that's one thing about him. He continues to make a billion mistakes and yes, I know. How many mistakes until we say enough is enough? But how much is enough for us? The mistakes are never the same ones. So, he is learning. Right? I guess the question now is if he's worth all the time, is he worth correcting, fixing and growing with? Yes, to me he was. In this absolute chaos, he accepts me yet breaks me apart. When he breaks me apart he fills in the emptiness with new perception, meaning and understanding.

Really Grace? Do you hear yourself? Justifying his actions by saying he is not perfect. By saying he is going to change. How many times must you repeat that lie to believe it? He slept with other girls. He maintained a complete relationship with someone else while with you. He says he just didn't know how to let go but obviously you weren't enough for him to want to let go. He stood out a day and can't remember what happened the night before. I bet you know what happened. STOP! Just stop. Please I can't stand the noise inside my head, and it's not voices, it's me. I can literally hear myself feeding all these thoughts to myself. Come on Grace, how much longer will you accept this. I'm afraid. I'm afraid to be alone. Not even "Lost Man" wanted me. Please STOP!

Get out of my head. I'm confused and I don't know what to do! You know what to do Grace. Leave. Get the fuck out before you lose you.

The tears begin. And again I hear you. Young girl, don't cry. This is only the beginning.

Sincerely,

Your friends, PTSD and Anxiety.

Chapter 9:

What have I done?

After all the bullshit I was finally in my own home. After my husband completely abandoned me for a week in that fucking shelter, and all the cheating he did. I thought I would never overcome it. I was finally home. Yet I still felt empty. The thought of being a cheater now ate away at me. But I couldn't stop thinking about Rob.

In the midst of all the drama Rob was my peace. Rob would call me every night before my husband got home, and we would just talk for hours. He was such a great listener. Rob knew all the right things to say to me. He kept me afloat, and I wasn't gonna let anything take that away from me. It was my time to be loved, and happy again.

One night Sara invited me out to celebrate her birthday. I was excited. We met up at a lounge, and Rob was there. Rob heard from Sara that I'd be there, so he decided to go. Matthew of course joined along as he was still trying to win my heart back. I was already long gone from ever loving him again.

As the night went on I bumped into one of Matthew's Ex-girlfriend. This was the same girl he previously cheated on me with. Even though I no longer cared for Matthew, something in me boiled up. I guess it was just knowing that I was face to face with one of the girls who broke our marriage. At first that's what I believed because she knew we were married, but honestly he destroyed our marriage. The girl didn't owe me a damn thing. She owe herself respect but clearly she didn't give a fuck.

I began taking shots after shots. I was so drunk, and had to get out of there. I literally wanted to beat the shit out of both of them. At one point Sara grabbed

me as she saw me getting closer to the girl. This bitch
had me exactly where she wanted me. Eventually I decided
that she wasn't worth coming out of character for so I
left.

We all headed to Sara's house. I felt hurt, and I
wanted nothing but to make Matthew feel what I felt. So
I did. I was breaking apart. So I gave Rob the look, and
that was enough. Rob knew exactly what was on my mind.
We went into Sara's bathroom, and had the most intense
sex I had ever had. I had no remorse.

Rob lifted my body onto the bathroom sink as he
kissed my neck. Rob rubbed on my chest, and down my
breast as our lips touched. Every second I wanted him
even more. His hands were so gentle as he lowered to my
thighs, and in between my legs. He removed my jeans as
he slowly came into me, and time just stood still as he
stroked gently in, and out. He continued kissing my
neck, and on my body. Up, and down our bodies just
became one. Even as I dripped with sweat my body

trembled, and chills ran down tickling my nipples, and legs.

Every second made me want him more. Rob's ear pressed against my lips as I moaned over, and over. We both released as his grip against my lower back tightened. We continued locking lips. His tongue against mine as we moved off the sink, and on to the toilet seat. It was a never ending train of euphoria. It amazed me how this man would stay rock hard, and wouldn't go down after rounds of cumming. Finally we finished. It was passionate, and hot as fuck. I wanted more.

Unfortunately I had to go back to reality. I had to face going back home to my husband. I no longer cared for him. I couldn't stand to be near him. Everything I once loved about him I now hated. The resentment only grew stronger each day.

The days went by, and the lies just kept swinging in through our door. Every weekend for about a month I'd lie. I'd say I was out when I was really in Rob's bed. I wanted nothing but to say I was in this hidden romance. I became who I despised the most. I was now Matthew.

Days passed, as Rob and I continued to communicate everyday. It became a routine of seeing him every weekend to every day, and wanting him more. Rob began making the darkness inside of me manageable, and easier to hide. The only problem now was Matthew. Things at home only began to worsen as things with Rob grew stronger.

I let myself go emotionally, and physically with Rob. After a month of lying, and hiding this secret I couldn't lie anymore. I think I only lied so I'd be able to have that escape whenever I needed it. So, I finally told Matthew I no longer loved him and it was because I had fallen for someone else. I told him about Rob.

Now I was the bad guy. I did exactly what broke me to someone else. I was supposed to love this man through thick, and thin. Who would have known that thick, and thin meant cheating after cheating for us. Where the hell did I go wrong? When did I let myself go? I never vowed to get cheated on or cheat back. When did I become someone I don't know? God, what have I done?

Chapter 9.5:

I don't love you like I did yesterday- battle #6
(The one I lost)

"I love you Grace." If you love me, then why? Why do exactly the same damn thing all the others have done. It was our first year anniversary, our first Christmas as a family together. How could you do this to me? You completely abandoned us. I was alone in that shelter. I had no contact with you. I was left on Read. I found myself talking to your answer machine over, and over again. All I wanted was to hear that you were okay. I'm sorry.

My stomach is turning. Paranoia from lack of sleep is taking its toll. All I wanted was for you to just come home. Crying myself to sleep every night. Even spraying your damn cologne over my pillow to pretend you were home. Why?

Pills became a friend to me now. Something to help me
ease this pain. Every swallow consumes my days. I fell
into this deep hole and soon ACS knocked on my door. I
couldn't even bring myself up to take the kids to school
for one whole week bro. What type of mother am I? How
could I let you control so much of my emotion? I gave
you too much fucking power.

You never loved me. If you did you would have respected
my mental illness. You knew how damaged I was. You
promised me lies, and blame me for hurting you. Again it
was my fault because I forgave you once, twice, and a
third time. Why would you, I mean how could you leave
us? This isn't me!

I let you back in out of desperation and I missed you. A
few days later I finally woke up from one of the
nightmares. You fucking bastard. How the fuck could you

tell her you love her again. I hate you. You say she means nothing to you, yet she was the one who ran across your mind when I was drowning. She was the one who was given "I love you's" while I lay awake in bed dying. In her arms you ran, while mine were empty.
You forgot about me when all I did was think of you. I dreamt of you. I wished, and even prayed for your return back home.

But you're here now, and I forgive you. So I thought.

The thoughts begin to consume me. Everytime you look at your phone I question who you're talking to. Everytime you come home late I pace and wonder if you're really alone.
I wonder if you're still telling her you love her.
"What if he's with her now grace?"
"No, he's not!"
I don't know how to take these thoughts out of my head.

So many lies and secrets from day one.
He had a whole other relationship for the first three
months of our relationship.
How can I trust someone again like this?
A man who destroyed your marriage after you stood
faithful and loyal.
Move on grace. It's your turn to have some fun. Why
should you stick around?
Why should you stay faithful any longer?

I can't keep this up any longer. This man swore to guard
my heart, and always protect me. I guess he didn't know
that meant emotionally as well as physically.
Yells turned into slamming, pushing into banging. Leave
him, you don't love him anymore. Why keep drowning?

These were the thoughts that consumed me. The thoughts
that pushed me. The thoughts that led me into the arms
of Rob.

Sincerely, PTSD.

Chapter 10:

This is now

I am no longer the girl I used to be. I've changed, but who wouldn't have? I was full of laughter, and joy. Now I wake up in total darkness wondering when I will awaken from this nightmare. It still feels as if I'm stuck in this black hole. Mom says all I need is prayer and faith in god, but how can I when I turned my back on him. I'm honestly ashamed. Now I'm just a hopeless, and lost soul.

Who will ever love me in this condition? It's hard to even love myself. My heart has been closed off, and even the excitement of love has disappeared. I hate it all, and all I want is to go far away, and never return home. I feel as if I'm living In emptiness. I've begun therapy once a week, and I still don't know what to feel or what to even think anymore. I'm one person once I step into that room, and another once I leave. I'm filled with antidepressants, anti anxiety pills, and fake smiles. What has become of me?

I know you're probably confused at this point. I'm going back a bit. My *PTSD* keeps replaying the cause of my cheating. Well, welcome to my world. This is me everyday. Hurricanes running through my brain. My past consumes my present, but of course I am to blame. We are all accountable for what we allow, and take in. Every single day I'm waking up to the same fucking routine. When will it end? It's time to try and get some sleep now. Pop another fucking pill.

One week later..

I woke up today and found the strength to finally let you go. You are gone. I woke up at peace, and found the strength to walk the kids to school. To get up from bed, and move forward. I can finally breathe again. I'm finally returning to normal. I learned that in order to be happy I need to love myself first. It's easier said than done, but not impossible. Each day that passes the pain lessens.

I'm okay.

Next week after..

Fuck you depression for keeping me a prisoner in my own home. You won't let me go out. Fuck you anxiety for clouding my judgement, and making me think he's out to destroy me. Fuck you PTSD for waking me up last night about 4 or 5 times. Thank you for making me scream each time, making it hard for me to breathe. You monster! Thank you for making me believe they are all out to get me, and there is no other option but to cut myself so I won't think of what you've done to me. Anxiety murdering my thoughts. Thank you.

I'm not okay!

I lay in a tub full of water. It's the only time I don't hear a damn thing. It's the only time I have a sense of peace. For an hour of my day the silence is golden. No one to respond to. No children calling out "Mommy, Mommy." When I don't even know who I am, how can I be a mommy? The pain is silenced as my head sinks underwater. I don't hear a sound. The voices are no longer telling me I am unworthy. Unworthy to be loved.

Chapter 10.5:

Not Sober Anymore- battle #7

How can I? How can I fight the urges to just feel this pain elsewhere? Somewhere other than my heart. It consumes me each and every day. I thought I could fight this, but it teases me, and calls my name for more. The feel of the blade running across my skin, it's a relief from what the fuck is going on inside of my head. How can I?

I left him, but my sanity is at its peak, I'm losing myself and there's no strength left in me. What the fuck am I doing anymore. This emptiness, when will it ever be filled again. Just do it Grace!!! Stop thinking and use me. I need this. Everyone is better off without you. You will never be enough for anyone. Don't believe what anyone says. I am your only friend. I've never failed

you. I've never judged you. I am always here. SHUT THE
FUCK UP! Get out of my head. Why am I so fucked up?

"This isn't You Grace. You are stronger than this
darkness. Don't let it consume you. Mom, and the kids
need you. They love you."

I can't live through this pain anymore. I'm alone. He
said it himself. No one will ever want me. I cannot be
loved. I am the problem. God, I feel so empty, and lost.
How could I possibly let a man have so much control over
me. Over my emotions. My head is now flooded with black
clouds. All I see is hate, pain, and fear. I can't give
up. They need me. They love me. I am worthy of love. I
am enough. I am strong. I will make it, and I will be
loved.
Depression, you will not win. I will cry, and I will
feel pain, but you will not win! Maybe someday in the
future you won't win. I need this pain to stop. I need

it to pour off my hands. I don't recognize who Grace is anymore. She's dead inside of me.

Sincerely,

Your Not so friend Depression!

Chapter 11:

Hello friend's

As you guys have read thus far my life has been pretty fucked up. I know you're wondering. How the fuck is she still surviving? Well here's how. I was diagnosed with PTSD in 2014. Fast forward to 2018, two more lovely friend's added to the gang. Anxiety, and Depression. Now I'm currently working on anger management. I have all this fucking anger built inside of me.

I mean yeah, I have built up anger, and at times it turns into aggression but I'm working on it. With me a simple argument can turn into a physical fight because of this built up resentment. I have this defense mechanism now because of all the men I allowed to fuck me up. Once they've crossed my personal space I snap easily. That's the fear I have of them hitting me. I'm only to blame.

Thankfully, therapy has taught me to take a step back and walk away. It doesn't always work but it's progress. When you remove the pain from your life it tends to become a little easier to cope with your diagnoses. My Anxiety has lowered but depression has really grown. Just the thought of being alone for the rest of my life haunts me. A lot of shit tends to haunt me nowadays. That's the Ptsd that's kicking my ass.

Post traumatic stress disorder is what really fucks with me the most. The traumatic events in my life are like a damn movie being played over, and over again in my head. Stuck on repeat. Any simple thing triggers my outburst, and I'm literally reenacting whatever traumatized me. I haven't really worked on that yet. I mean how can I escape it?

Depression is one lonely mother fucker. It brings you down so low into a ditch you can't climb out of. It's as if you're stuck in quicksand, and you just keep sinking deeper, and deeper. Each second gasping for air.

You're stuck in this darkness, and you can't find the light out of it. Your body tightens and weakens more, and more each day that passes.

Which then brings on the anxiety. You feel as if you can't breathe. As if you're dying, and there's no way out. Something inside of you is screaming to escape. It feels as if the world is crumbling down on you. Anxiety fills you with doubt, and fear. It tells you that you are not enough, and everything is against you. It tells you no matter what you do you can't escape it.

These are my friends, and who I live with everyday. I've had to live to accept them. There's no other way until I find the strength to leave them behind me. What other way? They'll just keep coming back. I wake up everyday, and don't even recognize who I've become. That girl in the mirror isn't me anymore.

My mind is now a prison with writings on the wall. "You will never be enough. You are not worthy. No one will ever love you. You are a failure. There is no way out." How could someone ever love me? I don't even love myself.

Chapter 12:

A familiar face

For the last 12 years of my life I've had this amazing friendship with my best friend Aria. Unfortunately, I never learned to stay consistent. I mean people always say we're in control of our own lives and emotions right? I wish I had control of so much more. I try fighting this feeling of abandonment in my life. Yet everyday I still wake up feeling alone.

When Aria invited me for a night out I basically seized the moment to rekindle our friendship. God, it was the best step in my life I have taken in years. Rekindling a friendship I needed to help keep me sane. Besides my mom, and cousin Nina, Aria was one of the greatest beings to walk into my life.

The thing about depression, and everything that comes along with it; is that it doesn't allow you to be happy. It doesn't allow you to have those who love you close by. It completely isolates you from the world. I never wanted to bring that negativity around others or even be a burden. I questioned if my presence was even wanted.

It's incredible to say that the one thing I needed the most was just a phone call away. Aria became my person. Aria kept me astray from the darkness from time to time that lingered inside of me.
When I cried, Aria cried. We literally can sit for hours, and just enjoy each other's company. Ok enough of the girl romance back to the chaos.

On the day of Aria's birthday party I gained a handful of surprises. I've been in, and out of Aria's life, and I realized that I missed so much time with her. It broke my heart just seeing all I've never experienced along her side.

The birth of her beautiful children which now I call my own nephews and niece. We opened up in ways we haven't before. That night I felt as if I gained a sisterhood with her. Even though in highschool she was already my sister. Even her family, they were now my family. Everyone welcomed me with open arms that night. Even a familiar face.

Tenn. Tenn was Aria's family member. We made a connection that night. Maybe it was because of everything I had experienced with Matthew but I was open to making new male friends now. For the first time I found a friend in which I could relate to. We shared kind of the same pain, and trust issues.

We had complications opening up at first. Well at least I did. I wasn't as interested in this long term friendship. Yet when we spoke it was as if we'd known each other for years. It's kind of funny how life works. I could see the hurt in his eyes, and he saw the pain in mine. After the party we spoke more, and more.

Of course we had our fears but that didn't stop us, life, and complicated relationships did. Our friendship didn't last much longer than about a month. Tenn was pretty open to his life story with me, and even cried at times. I could relate but of course like almost every male friendship I have it quickly turned into more.

Tenn wanted more. It was the first time a man has ever shown me his true feelings. It was something about his vulnerability that had me a bit drawn. I could see so much of myself in him. He understood me, and never judged what was creeping inside of my head. Or at least that's what I allowed myself to believe.

My mind slowly became consumed with the stories and wonders of the things that destroyed us. Wondering how a life with him would cross my mind more often than I wanted. I found comfort in not only Tenn but the lies that surrounded him. I wanted love, and a family who accepted me with flaws, and all. Tenn gave me that feeling of a family.

As beautiful as it began, in a glimpse it became just a shooting star. All there was left to do was wait. Would that shooting star land right in front of me? A wish waiting to come true. Just to have that sense of a family made me eager. Possibly being the reason why this feeling would soon turn into confusion.

I always believed that I found true love, but when Tenn came into my life that all changed. We confused it for love other than family. It caused an entanglement of lies, and drama to his home. He reminded me of the street love I once encountered. A brother from the hood.

So to smooth Tenn, I hope that this helps you find the strength to find your happiness. The strength to let go of your fear, and be freed. You are so much more than just a statistic. You are a shooting star waiting to shine. Just keep your dick in your pants and you'll get far. Not every girl you encounter has to be subject to a sexual connection. We all need a good friend we can relate to.

Chapter 12.5:

Wake me up when it's over- battle #8

Here I go again. Fighting this memory. I can see each moment replaying over, and over again. Another drunken night. Something to help soothe the pain. Just give me my pills. Anything to forget this life I chose to live. How hard is it to fucking leave? He keeps coming back because he says he loves me, and I let him. One night won't hurt as we'll sleep on our bed. It's not like I'll remember.

He climbs into bed, and tells me he loves me. Then begs to satisfy me just this once. He knows I'm drunk, and high. I say no, and start to laugh. For some odd reason it was funny to me how I couldn't speak clearly. He insisted on tucking me in, and I gave in.

He says I'm laughing so he knows I want it. Again, I say
no. My heart is racing as he sweet talks me, and I can
barely fight or breathe. My head is spinning, and yet he
removes my pants. The room begins to spin as his face
lays between my legs. He holds my legs wide apart, and
begins his seduction. I softly ask him to stop, and tell
him this isn't right.

"Please, stop. I don't love you anymore!" I can't love
you after the pain you've caused me.
He pauses, and looks up to me. I tell him to stop once
again as he glances at me with sad eyes, and I laugh
once more. What the fuck is so funny? For him it was a
sign to continue.
I say stop, but my body is weak and frail by the drugs
that consumed me.

I gave in, and soon reached climax. As I looked down his
pants were already off, and he was halfway into entering

me. I stopped him, and he continued. "Stop, I don't wanna do this." He forced a kiss on me to shut me up, and as I'm fighting to push him off me I scratched his face. He then slaps me. Holding me down by my neck I began crying. Suddenly I felt him in me.
Quickly stroking in, and out. As I'm laying there I realize I have no strength that matches his. So why do I even fight? I'm left staring at the ceiling while tears pour down my cheeks like a never ending rainfall. It must have been three minutes when he released inside of me and he finally realized what he'd done.
I argued, and his excuse was that he saw it in my eyes that I wanted it. That I am his and I'm supposed to want him.

How could you use this excuse to justify what you just did?
He manipulated me. Took advantage of me while I was weak. How is it possible the one man who swore to

protect me just became one of your worst fears. How
could you do this to me? You were supposed to love me!

The next day I awoke beside him. I was wet and
disgusted. Everything felt like a blur. I should've
never let him in. He had nowhere else to sleep, and I
gave in. I run to the bathroom and everything from
within me pours into my toilet bowl. Damn it! What have
I done? I kick him out, but before he goes he begins
another battle. Invading my privacy, and asking
questions. "Get the fuck out!" He then snatches my
phone. I black out.

"Hit him grace he just fucked you" the voice inside of
me says. My face is burning. It gets harder to breathe.
I swing at him, and punch him. "Give me my phone!" He
pushes back.
Everything happened so quickly. I hit him, and he hit
me. Suddenly he grabs me, and pulls me by my hair, as

he's trying to get me in the room. I'm fighting with all
the strength I have left from the night before.

I have nothing. He slams me against the wall banging my
head three times. Then grabs my neck, and as I'm trying
to fight him off he swings towards my face. I'm
scratching, and trying to kick him off. I'm yelling, "I
can't breathe." He starts yelling.

"You crazy bitch. That's why you will always be alone.
You are the problem, you delusional bitch. You wanted
this. You made me this way. Everything is your fault. No
one will ever love you, I hate you."

Each word punched a hole into my soul. Circling my
brain. It became a parasite that began sucking away at
me. Finally he got off, and ran out. All I could do was
cry. Aria. My person was ready to run to my rescue, and
so she did.

I ran into her arms, and broke down crying.

The man who made a promise to always cherish, and love me now became this monster. "It's your fault grace." How could you hurt him, and not just fix it? "What the fuck? Are you shitting me?" This is the man who tore me down, and broke me to a million pieces. "I can no longer think straight." I'm not myself anymore. I lost myself. Happiness is a stray in this darkness inside of me. I'm dying. I need to end this all.

Sincerely,

Your friend Ptsd

Chapter 13:

The End or beginning?

There's so much left to say, yet I'm lost at times, as if my mind is stuck in a box. In an empty room. I relate to my mind as a butterfly lingering to escape. Each time it attempts to leave it only gets burned little by little. Where do you even go from here? The first step of changing was recognizing my mental illness, and getting help. I continue to live in this circle of torment and misery because of the decisions I've made.

Loving others more than I love myself.
Putting others happiness before mine.
Sacrificing my dreams, and goals to become a wife.
Not letting go of toxic relationships.
and so much more.

In life we tend to set aside our power for a man. We believe that our whole world revolves around him in a marriage. Well it doesn't. Being married doesn't mean we should lower ourselves to raise them. A marriage is togetherness. You build him, he builds you.

We are stronger than we are taught to believe. Although It's been so hard for me to follow these words, I believe that when all else fails you are all you have. I was taught to love myself first because if you don't love yourself who else will? But I never followed that. I refused to believe that in this life there isn't someone out there that would love you the way you love them.

Now to catch you all up on my current situation. I live under a program given to me through the shelter. I lost it because of my failed marriage. When Matthew decided to think with his dick first, he got so caught up that he lost his job. No income, no voucher. Rent became unbearable on my own.

I won't be able to stay here much longer, but I've never been more ready to move on alone now. Funny how things work out. You're probably wondering what happened with Rob right? Rob, and I are still going. It's been incredible but something happened between us that made me distant with him. I wish I were able to get more into it but honestly it was a loss I don't think i'll ever be ready to write about.

I found love in Rob, and that I can say will never go away. Because of the hurt I unfortunately self sabotaged. I shut him out, and ran into the arms of another. You guys remember Paris right? Yea, that's who i turned to for comfort. I mean it's been easy. The man is locked up.

With Paris I never have to worry about getting hurt again. I could talk to him for hours without the fear of judgement. He sees me for me, and not my past. Paris knows of my darkness yet he still fell in love with me. I have someone to look forward to now. I have a future with a man that doesn't have any sexual ties with me. Paris fell in love with me without the sex being involved.

So, I let go of everything that had this hold on me. With Paris I can start over. I can be a new person. Paris helped me let go of the man I cheated on my husband with. He helped me escape the abuse. Now I am free. With my ex-husband being gone I can start a new life, and journey.

With police reports and an order of protection against my ex-husband I'm forced to hide in a domestic violence shelter. Being that he was under my lease he could return anytime. So, I took my children and left. I couldn't risk them witnessing anymore of the abuse.

I left home. All of the memories I've built with my children are now gone. All of my furniture and hard work are now gone. A piece of me was broken knowing I lost everything I built in my first home. All because of a failed marriage. I failed in providing my children a safe haven. I failed as a wife. Everything is gone.

Paris told me that this is just one door closing for a new one to open. New beginnings. So, as I began this story with drama, and pain. I will end it with comfort, and peace. This time I am eager because this is not the end but the beginning to a new life for my children and I. The beginning of a new journey, and romance. The beginning of my next story.

Saving Grace. Fin.

Index

Depression is a common but serious mental illness that affects people in a negative way. It takes control of a person's feelings. The way they think and act, but there is a way to cope with depression and it is treatable.

Anxiety is a feeling of worry, nervousness or being uneasy with an event or something that you are uncertain of its outcome. It is also Treatable.

Post Traumatic Stress Disorder (PTSD) develops after a stressing, or frightening event occurs, or a prolonged traumatic experience.

YOU ARE NOT ALONE!

In an event of a crisis please contact the following listed below: (NEW YORK CITY HELP LINES)

National Suicide Prevention Lifeline:
(800) 273-Talk (8255)

Safe Horizons Domestic Violence hotline:
(800) 621-Hope (4673)

Rape, Abuse, and incest national network (Rainn) sexual assault hotline:
(800) 656-hope (4673)

Call 911 in the event of an Emergency.

Thank you all for your support.